Hanging Around With BATS

By Lauren Weidenman

CELEBRATION PRESS
Pearson Learning Group

CONTENTS

THE TRUTH ABOUT BATS

Swarms of bats darken the sky as they leave their cave at dusk. What's going on? It's mealtime! These bats have just waked from a long day's rest. Now they are hungry. In one huge hunting party, they dart out into the evening air to search for their favorite food—insects.

Zipping through the sky in groups, bats look a bit like birds or insects. They are neither. Instead, they are **mammals**.

Bats leave their cave to search for food.

3

Bats are in the same group of animals as dogs and humans. They have hairy bodies and give birth to live babies. Baby bats, called pups, drink their mother's milk. In these ways bats are the same as other mammals. However, bats have one skill that no other mammal has—bats can fly.

Bats are special in other ways, too. They live almost everywhere on Earth except for the driest deserts and the ice-covered polar regions. There are almost a thousand **species**, or kinds, of bats! About 45 species live in North America.

Most people do not know what bats are really like. Others have some incorrect ideas about them. Bats are not dangerous. They are not blind or scary. They do not fly into people's hair or suck people's blood. They don't spread disease any more than any other wild animals do.

Fruit-eating bats help spread seeds.

The truth is that bats help people in many ways. Insect-eating bats help to control bugs that destroy crops and carry disease. Bats can gobble up to half of their weight in insects every night! Fruit-eating bats help to spread seeds and plant new trees.

There are no other animals quite like bats. You'll learn more about these gentle, night-flying creatures as you read this book.

BUILT FOR FLIGHT

Different species of bats can look very different from one another. Some are black, brown, gray, red, yellow, or white. Others are spotted or have brightly colored markings.

However, all bats have something in common. Their wings are the largest part of their bodies, and their bones are lightweight. These features make bats great fliers.

A red bat   A flying fox bat

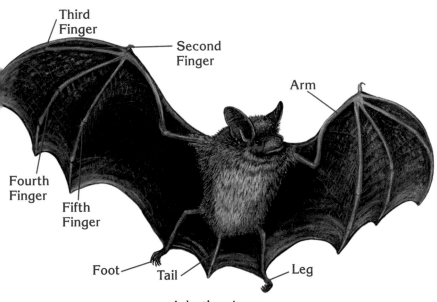

Third Finger

Second Finger

Arm

Fourth Finger

Fifth Finger

Foot Tail Leg

A bat's wings

Bat wings are different from those of birds or insects. The wings are made of thin skin that stretches between the bones of the arm and fingers.

When the wing closes, the bones come together. The skin is tucked away neatly between them. The bat's wing skin is also attached to the bat's legs and body. In some species, the skin connects the bat's legs to its tail.

A Mexican free-tailed bat

The lesser long-nosed bat feeds on the flower of a cactus.

Different kinds of bats have different-shaped wings. Bats that fly fast and far tend to have long, narrow wings. The Mexican free-tailed bat's long, narrow wings are just right for its nightly insect hunts and yearly trips south.

The lesser long-nosed bat, on the other hand, hovers around flowers and makes sharp turns in tight spots. Broader, shorter wings are better for its needs.

MEGABATS AND MICROBATS

Scientists have divided bats into two groups: **megabats** and **microbats**. Megabats are larger than microbats. Megabats can measure almost 6 feet across from wingtip to wingtip. They can weigh up to 4 pounds. Flying foxes are among almost 200 species of megabats. They live in warm, tropical areas in Asia, Africa, and Australia.

The flying fox is one kind of megabat.

Like foxes, megabats have large eyes and long noses. Their senses of sight and smell are sharp. This helps them find the fruit they eat. Besides fruit, some flying foxes also eat **nectar** and **pollen** from flowers.

Nearly 800 species make up the group of smaller bats—the microbats. The tiniest of these is called the bumblebee bat. Its body is about the size of a grape, and it weighs less than a penny.

All of the bats living in North America are microbats. One species of microbat, the little brown bat, is found throughout the United States and Canada. By day, these bats can be found sleeping in hollow trees, attics, caves, or other warm, moist shelters.

Like most microbats, little brown bats eat insects. One little brown bat can gulp down hundreds of bugs in an hour. Even more amazing, it catches them in the dark!

Bats send out sounds and listen for echoes.

How does a bat catch insects without seeing them? It **echolocates** (eh koh LOH kayts). This means that the bat makes high-pitched sounds and listens for echoes that come back. The echoes bounce off something such as an insect. This tells the bat exactly where the insect is. The echoes also let the bat know how large the insect is and how fast it is moving.

Bats send out the sounds through their mouths or noses. Some bats have special flaps of skin on their noses that help them direct the sounds. This flap is called a nose leaf.

All microbats echolocate, but most species of megabats cannot. Different bats use the skill in different ways. Echoes can tell a nectar-eating bat which flowers are full of pollen. Fish-eating bats listen for echoes bouncing off of a pond's surface. They can sense ripples in the water. They can even sense the back fin of a minnow sticking out above the pond!

Another reason bats echolocate is to find their way around in the dark. The streams of echoes give a bat a "sound picture" of its world. This helps it avoid bumping into things or flying in the wrong direction.

A Bat's Life

When they are not flying, bats hang upside down by their toes. A bat's resting place is called a roost. Most bats sleep during the day and are active at night. As a result they are careful to choose roosts that will keep them hidden from daytime enemies. Caves, holes in trees, openings in rocks and under bridges, and bell towers in churches all make good roosts.

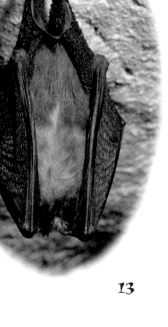

A bat's sharp claws help it cling to a cave wall.

Honduran white bats rest inside a leaf tent.

Bats are very skilled at finding safe roosting places. Some bats even make their own roosts. Honduran white bats chew tiny holes down the center of a leaf. This makes the leaf fold down and cover the bats like a tent. The bats cling to the leaf's stem by their toe claws. In this way they are hidden from view and are sheltered from rain and direct sunlight.

Some bats have different summer and winter roosts. Huge numbers of Mexican free-tailed bats spend their summers in caves in the southwestern United States. When winter comes, the supply of insects drops sharply. To find food, the bats travel, or **migrate**, south to Mexico or Central America. Some travel nearly 1,000 miles. Tropical fruit bats also migrate in search of food. They migrate to follow the fruits that ripen with each season.

Many bats that don't move to warmer climates **hibernate**, or go into a sleeplike state, for the winter. To get ready, a bat eats much more than normal. This gives the bat a store of energy that it uses as it sleeps. When a bat hibernates, its breathing and heartbeat slow down. Its temperature drops, too. In this state the bat uses less energy than it does when it is active.

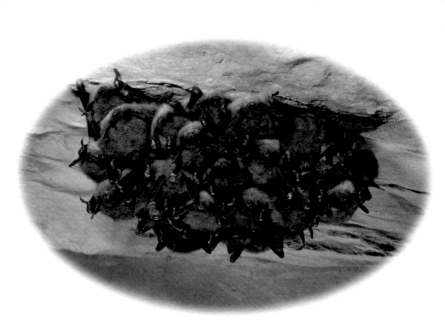

A group of hibernating bats

People must be careful not to wake up hibernating bats. Waking could cause the bats to use up their store of energy before the winter is over. Then, they could starve.

Huge groups of bats often hibernate together in the same cave. Therefore, not just one bat would die as a result of having been disturbed. Instead, thousands of bats might die.

BAT PUPS

Most female bats have a single pup or twins each year in the spring or early summer. Most microbat pups are born hairless and helpless. Megabats are born with fur and with their eyes wide open.

Mother bats take special care of their young. Little brown bats and Mexican free-tailed bats form nursery colonies, or groups of mother bats and their pups.

A bat pup clings to its mother.

Fruit bats carry their pups with them
when they hunt for food.

Each mother gets to know her pup by
licking its fur. There may be thousands of
pups in a nursery colony at a given time,
all crying at once. Yet, each mother knows
her own baby's voice and scent so well
that she can find her pup within minutes.

Most fruit bats do not leave their pups.
Instead, they carry them as they fly. The
pup clings tightly to its mother's fur, using
its claws.

BATS IN DANGER

One reason why bats are now in danger is that so many can be harmed at one time when they are hibernating. To protect the bats, signs can be posted at the entrance to caves or mines that are open. The signs can let people know that entering these places can harm hibernating bats.

There are other reasons why bats need our help. Many bats are losing their homes. People are cutting down forests at an alarming rate. As a result, bats that roost in trees now have fewer places to live.

Thousands of bats also lose their roosts when people close the entrances to caves and unused mines. Special gates can be put on entrances to help bats. The gates keep people and large animals out, but have holes large enough for bats to fly through.

Bats carry pollen from plant to plant.

Lesser long-nosed bats are in danger of dying out mostly from loss of homes and food and from being killed by people. These bats carry pollen from plant to plant, helping plants to make new seeds. Without the bats there would be fewer new plants.

There are other reasons why some bats are in danger. **Pesticides** used by farmers often poison their food. Many bats are killed by **predators**, such as hawks, owls, and snakes.

Bats help people by eating insects.

The good news is that people can help bat species that are in danger. First people need to learn more about the good bats do.

- Bats eat insect pests that destroy crops and carry diseases.
- They carry seeds that make new trees.
- They carry pollen from flower to flower, helping to make new plants.

If people know how important bats are, they might help to save these special creatures.

Bat houses provide places for bats to roost.

People can also help bats by giving them new places to live. One way is to make bat houses. Bat houses are a bit like birdhouses. They can be made in different shapes and sizes to attract different kinds of bats. Many people feel that having a bat house near their home is a great, natural way to keep insects under control.

Today there are many groups that work to spread the good word about bats and to help protect them. One of these is Bat Conservation International. The group sponsors programs to study and save bats. To find out more about how you can help bats, write to BCI at this address:

Bat Conservation International
P.O. Box 162603
Austin, TX 78716-2603

Learning about bats

GLOSSARY

echolocate to send out streams of high-pitched sounds and use the echoes that bounce back to tell where an object is

hibernate to go into a sleeplike state

mammal an animal with a backbone and hair or fur; mothers produce milk for their babies

megabats large, fruit-eating bats that live in warm, tropical regions in Asia, Africa, and Australia

microbats smaller bats that live in cooler climates and eat mostly insects

migrate to move from one region or climate to another

nectar a sweet liquid in many flowers

pollen a fine, yellow powder on part of a flower

pesticide a poison used to kill insects or other pests

predator an animal that hunts and kills other animals for food

species a group of living things that are alike in certain ways